For Joe, Alex, Anna, Simon, Mary and Clare who are my inspiration.
For Gary Craig, EFT founder whose unending curiosity and desire to
help others developed these wonderful techniques. - GMFM

ISBN: 10- 1481289586
ISBN: 13-978-1481289580

While EFT has produced remarkable clinical results in treating
physical and psychological issues, not everyone will respond in the
same way. Gail Mae Ferguson-Maceda is not a doctor and any
information herein is not intended to diagnose, treat or replace
your doctor's care. This book is to introduce you to EFT (Emotional
Freedom Techniques) and although EFT has no documented
negative side effects, you must take responsibility for your own and
your child's well being. If you have any concerns, please contact
your doctor prior to using the techniques.

# John Taps Away The Blues

Gail Mae Ferguson-Maceda

Illustrations by Manoj Vijayan

Last week at school, the kids in Ms Summer's third grade class were rehearsing for the school's dance performance. John was dancing his part in the performance when Marco, Lisa and Nasir all made fun of him. He was having the best time, really letting go and rocking and he felt scared and embarrassed when they made fun of him.

John thought to himself, "How could I be so stupid to have done that? Why didn't I realize what I was doing? I must have looked so stupid for them to laugh at me like that."

John started to feel really bad and when his Mom, Sadie, picked him up at school that day, he was grumpy and irritable and his Mom didn't know why.

After they picked up his little brother Alistair from Kindergarten, the trio went home for an after school snack and some play time in the park.

When they arrived home John didn't feel like playing, he went to his room and plopped on his bed.

Sadie came in to see if he was okay. Was he sick or was he upset about something?

Alistair was concerned too and came in to the room to see if his brother was okay. Sadie told Alistair that he could watch a movie or play in the backyard or living room while she checked on John.

Moms have intuition (that means they have a knowing feeling) when it comes to their kids and Sadie sensed something was wrong, that something had upset John. So she sat on the edge of the bed and said, "What's up, John? Did something happen at school today?"

John just buried his head in the pillow further. He was almost going to cry and he was afraid that if he let go and cried, he might just fall apart. Sadie started to pat his back and say, "It's okay, everything is going to be okay". Hearing those words John just melted and his tears fell.

Sadie asked, "What happened?" and John sat up and told her what happened at the rehearsal. She held him while he cried some of the sadness out and then she said to him, "Would you like to tap some of that sadness out?"

11

Now John knew what that meant. His Mom had often tapped with him before and he always felt better when she did and he liked it. So he readily agreed. Sadie knew this special way to make people feel better by gently tapping on some points on the body. She gently tapped on the side of his hand and she said,

"Even though I have this sad feeling in my heart, I am still a great kid.

"Even though I have this sad feeling in my heart, I am still a wonderful boy.

"Even though I have this sad feeling, I am going to be okay."

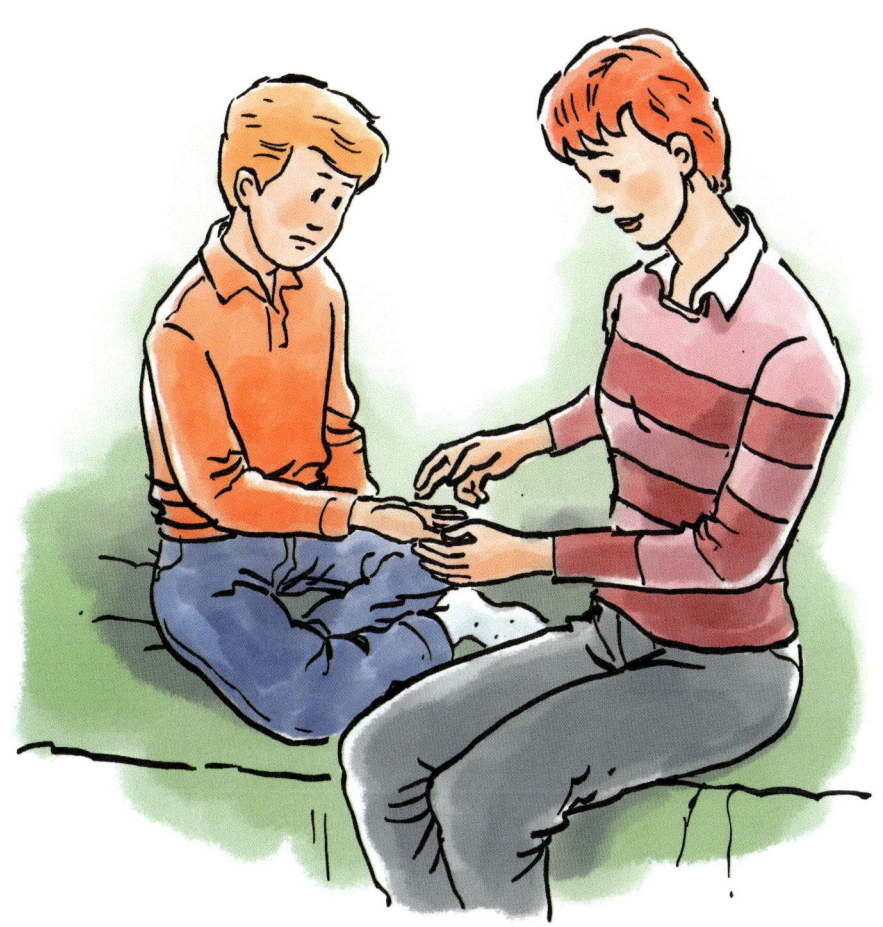

13

John started to feel better already.

When bad things happen, people can go into a bit of shock. They get scared and their energy flow gets stuck. When we tap, it unblocks the stuck energy. The energy starts to flow again and we feel better.

John still wasn't feeling completely better yet so Sadie kept tapping on some other points on his body like the top of his head,

14

the corner of his eye,

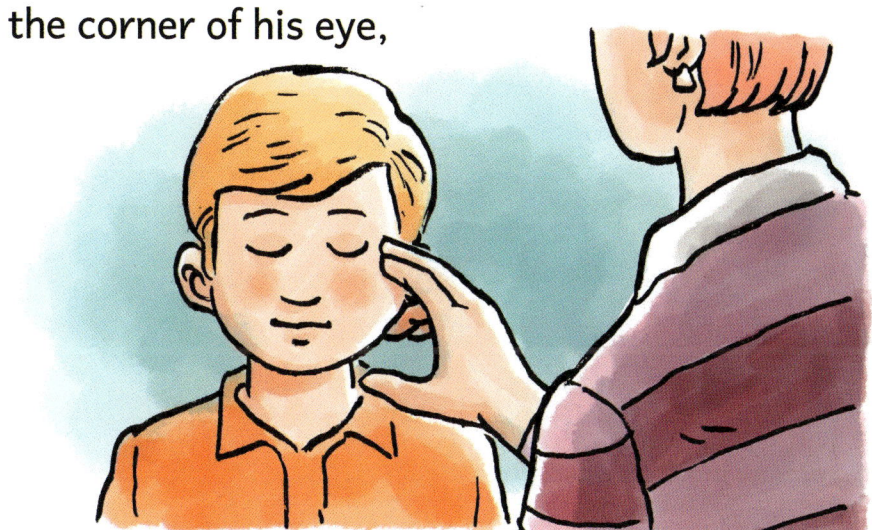

and under his collarbone.

Then Sadie had him take a deep breath and he knew he was feeling more like his happy self again.

Sadie asked him how he was feeling now and he said, "I am feeling much better now Mom. I'm not so sad anymore but I am angry at Marco, Lisa and Nasir for making fun of me. How would they like it if someone made fun of their dancing?"

Sadie agreed with John and asked him to guess what number between 1 and 10 did he think his anger might be? John said an, "8."

"Okay, an 8," said Sadie. "Would you like to tap that anger away, John?" John agreed that yes, he did. He didn't like that feeling and he didn't want to be angry at his friends. Besides, he wanted to go and have some fun in the park with Alistair.

So Sadie tapped on the side of his hand again. "Even though I feel this anger, I'm still a great kid.

"Even though I have this angry feeling, I'm still a cool kid.

"Even though I have this anger, everything is going to be okay."

By this time John was tapping on himself while Sadie tapped on herself. John knew the tapping points too.

So while they tapped on the top of the head, they said, "This anger."

After doing a round of tapping on all the points, John took a deep breath, which was easy because he wasn't feeling angry anymore.

After the round, John looked at his Mom and said, " You know Mom, I'm not angry at the them any more, I just think they didn't know what they were doing and now I don't care if they thought my dancing was funny or not. I had a great time anyway.

"Maybe I'll be famous one day as the Funny Dancing Man and people will come to see me dance because it will make them laugh. I would like that!"

"Thanks Mom, I love you," said John, as he gave his Mom a big hug. "Can Alistair and I go to the park now?"

# How Energy Flows in our Body

Just like John tapped on his bad feelings and felt better very quickly, you can too! Everything in this wonderful world including you is made up of energy. Energy flows through our bodies similar to how electricity flows through an electrical wire. When you turn off the lamp at home it cuts off the energy flowing to the lamp, and so there cannot be any light.

# JOHN TAPS AWAY THE BLUES

In our bodies our energy flow can be cut off or limited too. It might happen from an accident or a broken arm. It can also happen when someone hurts our feelings, or when we get scared or get disappointed over something. It happens to everyone and in some cases if you don't clear the bad feelings, your energy can get stuck and not flow as well as it should. Then you just don't feel as happy.

Sometimes later on people can get sick too because their energy (life force) is so weak.

Let's look at the lamp again.

What happens if there is a crimp in the electrical cord? The lamp may flicker on and off or come on and then off again. The lamp's light is not as bright as it could be.

This is what can happen to us too. Tapping gets our energy working at its best and flowing as it should be so we can feel healthy and happy. It's so easy to do.

26

Here is a chart showing where to tap. You only need to tap about 4 to 9 times very gently on each point while you say out loud how you feel. Just like John did. And if you want to tap without anyone knowing, you can tap on your fingers under your desk at school, or when you are in the bathroom. You can also just hold a tapping point and take a deep breath and no one knows that you are tapping!

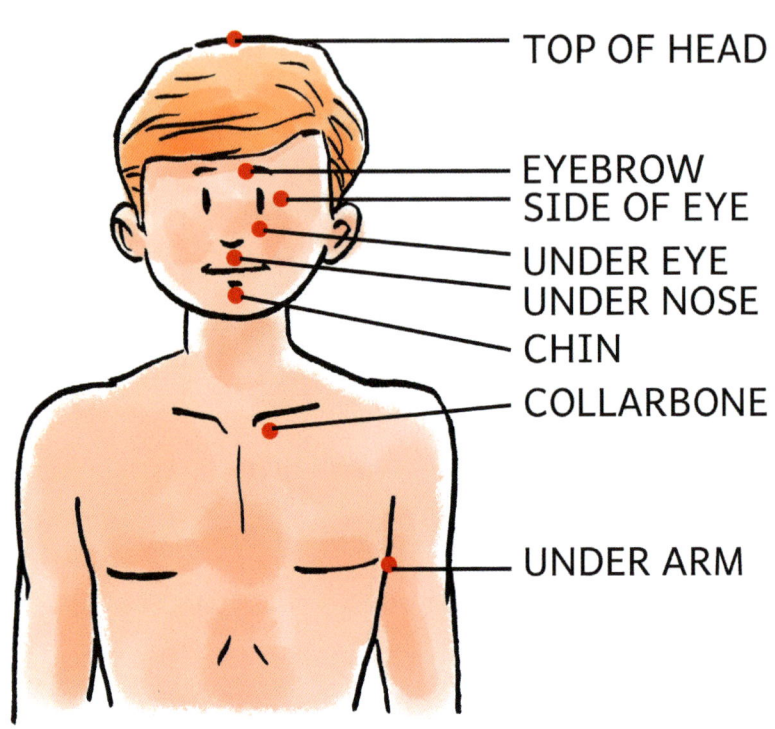

TOP OF HEAD

EYEBROW
SIDE OF EYE
UNDER EYE
UNDER NOSE
CHIN
COLLARBONE

UNDER ARM

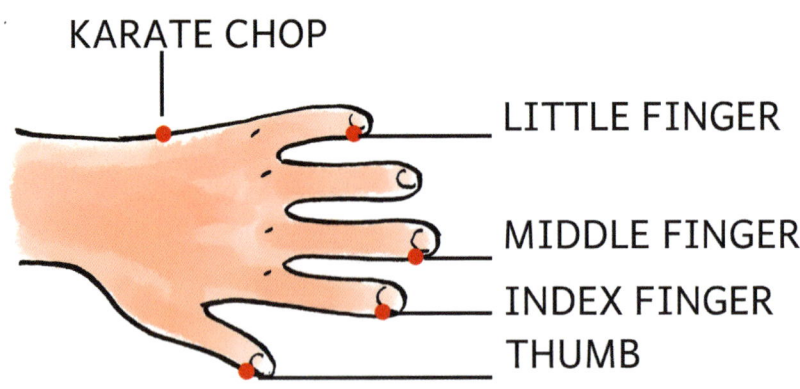

KARATE CHOP

LITTLE FINGER

MIDDLE FINGER

INDEX FINGER
THUMB

This same energy runs through the whole world. In China the doctors have known about and worked with energy flow in the body for 6,000 years. Here's a picture showing the meridian pathways, through which energy flows in your amazing body.

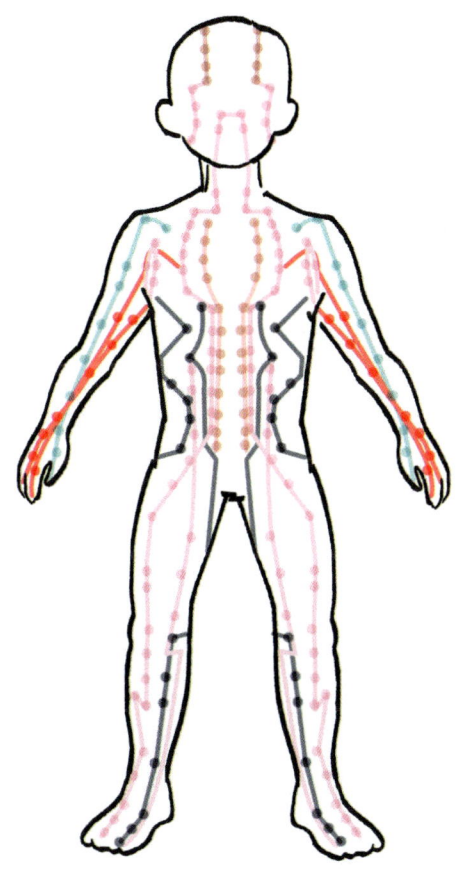

# How to Tap

To begin, think about your problem and your feelings about it and give it a number between 1-10. Just like John rated his anger at his friends at an 8. If you don't know what the number is that's okay, just take a guess and it will still work.

Perhaps you are feeling scared, frustrated, confused, sad, disappointed, angry, alone, misunderstood or worried. There are a lot of different feelings we can have.

Sometimes our feelings might feel like "butterflies in our stomach", or you might be so scared that your "legs feel like lead."

Your feelings and thoughts are energy too and when you tap they can change pretty fast. Just like they did with John.

Start to tap on the Karate Chop point first and state your feelings three times at the beginning with these words, you can add some of your own words, as long as you are stating the negative feeling first with "Even though" and then following with a positive statement after.

Put your feeling in the blank space.

"Even though I have this _____feeling, I am still a great kid.

Even though I have this _____feeling, I'm still a lovable person.

Even though I have this_____feeling, I am a good person and it's okay to have these feelings."

Then tap around all the points in a sequence starting at the top of the head stating the problem or feeling each time.

| | | | | |
|---|---|---|---|---|
| 1.Top of Head | TH | 5. Under Nose | UN |
| 2. Eyebrow Point | EB | 6. Chin | CP |
| 3. Side of Eye | SE | 7. Collar Bone | CB |
| 4. Under Eye | UE | 8. Under Arm | UA |

Continue with the finger points starting at the thumb.

Repeat the sequence starting at the TH and continuing on all the points until that negative feeling goes down to a 0.

A new negative feeling may come up so you would tap that one down to a zero too, starting at the Karate Chop point first until you are feeling that there is no problem anymore and you are feeling good again.

# For Parents and Caregivers

As a Mom of five kids, I wish that I had known about EFT years ago when my kids were young. Firstly, because it would have helped me tremendously as a parent in dealing with my frustrations, worry and decision making but also it would have helped my kids navigate through life so much more easily.

There is much you can find about EFT online, either through my website or many others sites. It is a wonderful self help tool developed firstly by Dr Roger Callahan, when it was called TFT (Thought Field Therapy) and later refined by Gary Craig and called EFT (Emotional Freedom Techniques). EFT is based on the ancient Chinese acupuncture meridians on the body. The Chinese believe that pain, disease and emotional problems can be caused by a blockage in the energy system. In EFT we tap on only a few of these points while talking about the problem or issue. Gary Craig says "you can tap on everything", meaning any emotional issue, relationship, pain, addiction, post traumatic stress disorder (PTSD) and disease. Everything!

The wonderful thing about kids is that their energy system is so strong and their "issues" are not as deep seated as ours are, so they clear very quickly, just like John did in the story.

Sometimes my youngest would come home upset about something, perhaps her sister had been mean to her or a friend had snubbed her at school. If she didn't want to be tapped on, I would tap on myself while she talked about the problem. I would just listen and empathize and tap, within 2 minutes she was off and running, issue resolved and forgotten about. It can be that quick.

Another neat thing to do with kids at night if they can't sleep or they have a worry, just tapping on their spine or rubbing their spine (there are meridian points there too) can help them relax and fall asleep.

There is also a wonderful tool that EFT practitioners have been using with children called the Tappy Bear developed by Till Schilling. If you cannot find a Tappy Bear you can take a stuffed toy bear and have the child tap on the bear's EFT points. The child is then dissociated from the problem being 'theirs' and before you know it the "bear's" problems are all gone! Please see my book, "A Day in Kindergarten with Alistair, Sebastian and Mr Arroyo."

Picture Tapping Technique is another wonderful EFT technique (a combination of EFT and Art Therapy) developed by Philip Davis and Christine Sutton from the UK. The kids draw a simple picture of their problem and then we tap on what was drawn on the picture.

It is my dream to get EFT in the schools to help kids to be less stressed and more at ease, and therefore able to learn better. EFT can help them with test anxiety and scores, sports, all academic areas and extracurricular activities. It has also proven effective with ADHD and allergies.

Even though John's problem may not seem like a huge trauma, if situations like this recur, it may cause him to have a subconscious fear of speaking or performing in front of people. This can create problems later in life, limiting his career choices and job performance, causing anxiety and stress. Sadly in some cases kids can have larger traumas such as sexual and physical abuse, divorce, death of a loved one, car accidents, alcoholic or drug addicted parents and life threatening diseases. For these cases I suggest looking for an experienced practitioner.

I encourage you to learn more about this

wonderful self help tool. Please don't hesitate to email me if you have any questions. My mission is to help people to reach their full potential so they may make a positive difference in the world. With EFT we can help get kids off to a good start early in life.

# Nutrition and Exercise

A couple of last things to mention is the importance of both a healthy diet and exercise for your child. I can't go fully into the science and chemistry of the negative impact of what junk food does to the body and brain, that is another book. But I encourage you to study the effects for the sake of your child. As their bodies and brains are developing they need optimal nutrition. Junk food has been proven to not only cause behavioral issues but also underachievement and obesity. When fresh, healthy, organic food is taken into the body, the result is a happy, more vibrant and fully alive child.

This brings me also to the importance of exercise. Not only has exercise all the physical value of strengthening muscles and bones, oxygenating the blood etc. but also releases endorphins in the brain to give the child a sense of calm and relaxation.

I wish you only the best on your journey of love and parenthood. You have the privilege of making a difference in the world by your light and love shining in your child's life.

email: info@gailmae.com
website: www.gailmae.com

# Links

www.gailmae.com

Gary Craig's website:
http://www.emofree.com/eft/?aft=670

A very good article from Patricia Carrington's
website explaining the history of EFT:
http://masteringeft.com/masteringblog/about-eft/
history-of-eft/

Picture Tapping Technique Website:
http://www.picturetapping.com/index.php

A good article of the Effect of Nutrition on
Children's Behavior from Till Schilling:
http://www.tappybear.com/does-diet-affect-your-
childs-behaviour/

An excellent book of Tapping Scripts especially written
for children from Sue Jeffrey Busen:
http://www.tapintobalance.com/products/tap-into-joy/

A resource for stuffed toys with the tapping points on them.
http://www.feelbetterbuddies.com/

# About the Author

**G**ail Mae Ferguson-Maceda is an Advanced Level EFT and Matrix Reimprinting Practitioner living and working in New York City. Formerly a ballerina with the Australian Ballet Company, a performer on Broadway in "A Chorus Line" and Bob Fosse's "Dancin", a teacher and choreographer, her greatest career and joy is as a Mom of five kids. She sees clients all over the world on Skype as well as in person in the New York City area, gives talks and holds workshops on the benefits of EFT, Matrix Reimprinting and other energy therapies. She believes that the future of the world is in the hands of our children and it is our responsibility to create a safe and healthy world for them to grow up in. The best way to do this is to achieve a personal physical, emotional and spiritual balance through EFT and other energy modalities.

43

Printed in Great Britain
by Amazon